Ohigan
the other shore

Poems

Like butterflies, they fly about
and mesmerize —
                    flutterings
of feelings —

often in-discernible,

until
at last (perhaps) one lands

a kiss
upon your finger —

Table of Contents

Introduction

As you're reading this book of poetry, my hope is that the theme of passage through change and transformation will emerge. I took pains to order the poems in such a way that, in the end, the order in which you read them will make no matter; hopefully the theme will come through regardless.

While the poems are original, and of both lesser and loftier significance, the theme of transformation is serious—and an unavoidable cliché. Poetry often displays the annoying tendency toward acting that way—taking itself too seriously—and these poems run that risk.

Within the theme (and experience) of change and transformation, there's an alchemy at work. It creates an embarrassment of writing richness. When I wrote and assembled my poems within such a serious cliché, I attempted to own it as a defiant form of play—to just put it all out there, and, at the end of the day, all I want to do is play along the pathways I travel, just like when I was a child. Like a child, I am wearing my insides on the outside through these pages.

On the first anniversary of my father's death, I stumbled online into the Japanese word "ohigan." Ohigan, meaning "the other shore," is a weeklong Japanese national holiday which occurs twice a year, during the autumnal and vernal equinoxes. During the equinox weeks of Ohigan, the Japanese traditionally take the time to pause, reflect, and remember their ancestors. Gravesites are cleaned, prayers are lifted, offerings of fresh flowers and food are made.

Since the first anniversary of my father's death, I have adopted ohigan as a practice in my life. Twice a year, on the equinoxes, I give myself the simple gift of taking dedicated time to reflect on my loved ones (deceased and alive), and I quite naturally become self-reflective. In this book of poems, I attempt to share some of the essence of my reflections on my own small and large journeys of change. The writing has been helpful for me. Sharing my poems always makes me feel less alone in the world. My hope is the reader finds the poems helpful, and somehow less alone in the world as well. At the very least, I hope the poems cause the reader to raise a quizzical eyebrow from time to time.

Dedicated to my father, John Harold Fairchild.
(9/27/1938–9/13/2017)

Wonder

One foot falling
after one foot falling,
I ascend into the
wonder of wilderness
in winter.

When I reach the boulder fields
they seem to tumble
in slow motion.
The rocks, at rest, are full of
movement
too slow to detect.
       Do the rock-lichen know?

In the alpine meadows,
playfully braiding
rivulets of water flow
through red heather,
golden grass and
green spongy moss.
An amphibian's paradise.
       Do the polliwogs know?

Further up, snow falls.
A silent offering, an invitation to
consider coldness and austerity.
A blanket of white snow
wraps around an alpine lake,
feeding the meadow's life,
feeding me.
       What do I know?

The Urge To Bloom

Running within
Braids of flowers
Woven through
Alpine meadows,
Hugging edges of
Small streams
Flowing from
Snow still tucked up high.

Snow releasing into
Streams flowing into
Grottos of plant life.
Green and blue,
Yellow and red, and
Still more yellow
Can't resist the
Urge to bloom.

The urge to bloom
So much more
While running within
Alpine meadows
Woven with
Braids of flowers.

Puzzling

When I was a child
I played in dreamtime,
running through suburban
backyards searching for clues.

I pieced and puzzled
a world into reason.
I shaped meaning
out of randomness.

I   had   no   say   in   becoming.

Armed with the certainty
of a religious order,
my childhood dreamtime
shaped the boundaries of my ego.

Swirling within a black hole of self-absorption,
I emerged from my certainty beyond
suburbs of thought and into wider,
more curious ways of being.

In a good time, the distance from
that black hole increased.
The swirling slowed,
And an illusion of lucidity gained.

What was certain is unreliable.
What was refined is weathered,

The puzzle of reason remains.

Porthole

Lying in a green field,
Naked to the sun,
A warm breeze
Soothes my soul.

Through a porthole of light
A medic's voice—
"Mr. Fairchild . . . you are
Having a heart attack."

It all changes—everything
changes—from green to
black to white to green to
black, swirling back and back
again.

Flashing light
All around.
Whirling sound
All around.

What does it mean if
nothing more matters?
Who am I if not the
self of who I was?

Who will I

The Frontier

Sitting on the frontier.
The edge of the known—the edge
of the unknown.

Just beyond the suburbs, where houses
stretch thin with increased
distance between them.

Up and to the edge
of human development.

There—and just beyond—
forests where no
tree has ever been touched,
no blade scarred into the earth.

On that frontier
anything happens
all at the same time.
The birds sing,
pinecones fall
to the forest floor,
cottonwood seeds
sparkle in the air.

Timeless synchronicity, and yet

there can only be
that one thing
that happens
next.

An ancient always-place: Being.
This is the wild place:
Frontier.

Today's Awareness

Straining to see around the river's bend
Through thick cover beyond dim light,
My age, my lot, timing, relationships
Culminate in today's awareness.

What I thought I knew was wrong.
The control I possessed—an illusion.

Simply:

Love deeply.

(You're on your own)

Ride life's rapids with
A semblance of style.

Spacious

I carve a nook
off to the side of well-traveled
pathways of thought.

I prepare the nook, a comfortable perch from which to
watch the world,
and breathe.

Clearing the roughage of culture,
I don't stop until the thought
beneath the thought,
the essential feeling, is revealed.

Feeling the shape of emotion,
I reason it into form
on the surface of thought.

In stillness, the form is released to flight.
Watch the world
and breathe.

Bacteria by Billions

*Jim Harrison: And then you can sense the craziness
of the genome, or that each cell of a willow tree has
nineteen thousand determinates. In each cell of
what that willow tree is, everything becomes vivid,
you know? The birds, my brain, the birds looking at
me, me looking at the birds. Nature becomes totally
holographic that way.*

Gary Snyder: Now you can write haiku.

*Jim Harrison: It just enlarges the conception of life.
If you know that a teaspoon of soil has a billion
bacteria in it, for example—*

Gary Snyder: So how do we put that into a poem?

—from *The Etiquette of Freedom*,
edited by Paul Ebenkamp

And here I am, within no one else.
Resting by a lazy stream
In the heart of
MOUNTAINS so high
The sun doesn't
Kiss the skin
Until 10am.

Bacteria by billions!

Everywhere I look, listen, and feel: a bug!
Then a snake, a frog, a fish,
Chipmunk, moth
And mosquito.
My son runs from one to the next
All gibberish and words of amazement.

With my eyes

Bugs buzz by
Insects crawl
Water moves
Plants puffy & verdant
Swell with life
Flowers flex their blooms
Patterns puzzle in bark of
Cedar, Hemlock, and Fir
With my ears

Bugs buzz
Waters ripple
A hummingbird hovers
Inspecting my scribble.
Leaves shudder and hush
A frog clucks then croaks
And branches snap/break
Under unknown forces

Within my body

Bugs tickle my arm
I walk up the skin
Life is electric within it.
Then...
Hover buzz above
Hop on a rock
Be tall, stately, and slow
Nibble kibble of
Pine and needle
Slither through
Blade and cone

Bacteria by billions!

Connect
to it all...

Bacteria by Billions! *Short(er) Form*

Everywhere I look, listen, and feel, a bug!
Bacteria by billions
And here I am,
With my eyes
With my ears
Within my body.
Bacteria by billions
Connect
Me
To it all.

Haiku!

Everywhere I look
Bacteria by billions!
All to connect it—

Surfacing Gratitude

There are so many
   reasons to be here
      in this present moment,

        sitting secluded under the giant maple trees
   stretching up into the morning,
arms outward to the sky.

The leaves! The leaves, green handprints on clouds!

From the tree beside me to another and
   another, lit-green handprints
      interlock together.

      Spongy mosses, soaked in Spring's
   glistening moisture,
extend their slow sprawl up and out,

and trilliums emerge, firm from stem
   to three-leaf ruff, thrice smiling,
      spreading imperfect petal symmetry.

My God! How proud the trillium petals hold their glory!?

      Maidenhair ferns of royal splendor
   caress the nape of
the slender space between their leaves.

Woven water falls through the
   purr of hummingbird, buzz of bee,
      chickadee, chickadee, and a baritone hoot—

      The moment, grateful,
   arises on the surface from
curiosity's green tendrils—

Golden Green

It's in moments like these,
When the water's flow
Captures me
In rippling sound waves,

When the morning thrush
Pirouettes in time,
Perching on the anvil
Of my ear,

When golden green rays shine
Through windows in the canopy
Illuminating chosen ferns on
The forest floor,

That the courage to give away
All my money intoxicates me
And seems to be the
Most rational thing I can do.

Natural Flow

You are sitting just above a stream, and
Listening to water flow.

The wind dances on your skin, and
Gently tickles tremoring licorice ferns
Up the spine of a mossy maple tree.

Sound and movement harmonize
Within birdsong swirling
In the sprite morning air.

Feel this wilderness
Within you
Let it carry you
Throughout the day.

My Hands

Hold the carpenter's pencil.
They grip the worn wheel,
button the ripped jeans,
pull the faded shade,
and scratch behind the dog's ear
to feel the softest fur on her body.

Tool makers,
tree climbers,
homebuilders,
back scratchers,
my hands build whatever needs building.
They tousle
my son's
floppy red hair.

The Beauty of Love

Love manifested the instant she saw her:
flies circling the stray dog sitting
on the morning's golden doorstep.

My daughter poured her heart
onto the dog,
named her Princess, and
Princess received the
total of my girl's affection.

We saw through her mangy skin, and
the ribs we could count, and
the scabs on her snout,

Princess became polished and plump,
the apple of my little girl's eye.

Beauty within beauty, love within love.

Waterfall Creek

Standing upon the bridge
As my children troll beneath,
The water falls between us,
Through the earth, and all of time.

Water from the indigenous past.
Water in bear, coyote, owl, and deer.
Water In the fern, the moss,
Trees, and berries.

Swelling wet,
Within a blue drop,
Against the black
Speckled space.

We are only but for water
Floating and falling through
This waterfall creek, as I stand above
And my children troll beneath.

Love's Continuation

Sunlight shines
through the canopy.
Maple trees wavering
in florescent green.

A flowing wave,
this life, this one life.

The frozen tips of
ponderosa pine
needles sparkle in the
morning sunlight.

Shining love
into my children.

Now the setting sunlight
glows on the horizon
above an expanse
of deepening blue.

Love continues
through my children
—through us all
Love continues—

Love Angels

Snow falls outside the window.
Quiet and light.
Winter descends.

Sitting beside my son
In front of a warm fire,
I read and consider a book
On heritage and ancestry.

I look up, and
In a shared moment,

We look into each other, and
He smiles at me.

Does my son know
We are an extension of love,
One and the same?

Does he know we are connected
By the quiet light of love softly
Descending through the bodies of the ages

To land on our hearts and
Make angels within?

We look into each other, and
I smile at him.

A Good Yearning

Sometimes it is the glimpse
Of a dream I remember
Upon waking that moves me
As tears pull to be let free.

Papa! Papa! Papa!
My son calls to me
Through some unknown chaos.

And then I am wide awake, upright
Rocking with that weight
Held tightly in my arms,

Yearning for my father,
Yearning for my son, a good
Yearning for my soul.

A Life Lesson

Morning after morning,
When I was five,
I ran down
Our long gravel drive,
Following my seven-year-old
Sister-guide.

At the end of the drive
Stood an apple tree
With branches stretched
For us to climb.

One misty morning
We found two
Baby birds tucked
Into a rotted knot.
Warm and safe siblings
With mouths open wide,
Cozy there for us to find.

Morning after morning
I ran down
Our long gravel drive
Following my guide, and
We climbed the tree to see.

Until one morning
We didn't find the
still flightless siblings, and
We climbed, curious, down
To the ground.

Ways to Be

From the half-lit corner, I watch you pretend not to
observe us, the older men. You're pretending
not to listen, pretending not to study our moves.

Something holds you back on the edge of light.
Is it helpful to hide there, in plain sight?
Are you comforted by the idea of not being seen?

As if we don't see you, as if we don't know how you feel.
Youth, viewing its future self, considering, yes,
I feel you feel your men laugh, my son, I see you learning
ways to be.

Heartbreaker

I know it's risky.
I know the danger.
Loving so deeply
means heartbreak,
separation, loss.

But I can't help myself,
watching my daughter
walk out the door to
school—through
the window I watch her trot
up the stairs, down the street,
out of sight.

My heart inflates,
my eyes water—the pain of
love's longing.
Every time my sweet girl
walks away
the pain seeps in.
I know, I know, I must
feel it, and let it go,
let it go, let it go
let her go—

Holding Innocence

The fresh sword fern
in the spring forest

is innocence itself, its
damp curls.

I lie inside it,
a cover of soft down,

and curl around my son as he curls
around his teddy bear.

(Protected, we leaf, and
leave uncurling for later.)

Eyes closed,
we fall asleep.

ohigan

Dying
Experience
He said he wanted
To experience his death

Palms down on the white
Fruit-of-the-Loom t-shirt
Of his passage

I softly beat the stained
Drumskin of his heaving chest

Do you feel, Father?
Do you feel me now?
You're passing, Father
Oh I love you

You mouthed–I love you–in return

The last tearful touch
The other shore calling
And then–you were
Gone from sight

His crossing began when
His Alzheimer's crept in

And for a time he knew
And then he forgot the
Fording began long ago

His death experience
Now sown within
Me to give me
Living

dying

Paternal Parting

I was five years old playing
In the basement rec-room.

A swing-set built inside by my father's
firm hands holding on for a time.

My sister floated into the room and
told me it was my turn to say goodbye.

And there I was on the landing
by the front door of our split-level farmhouse.

My father, resolute, with luggage on either side,
loomed next to me.

I have no memory of our words,
just his fingers through my hair.

And then he left me on the landing, and
walked out the front door into a waiting taxi.

I turned and ran back downstairs,
into the wrecked room of my memory.

I told myself out loud, to my sister, "I don't care."
And swung until my toes touched the ceiling.

Sweet
Sweet Mom

Always on the move, my mom.
She had to hustle just to clothe us.
Wrapped in warmth within our home,
I often felt her efforts arduous.

I lived within her struggle,
Knowing my role was to please.
I helped her in her hustle
And sought her loving praise.

At times she cried in bed at night,
While I sat there beside her, and
Simply squeezed her hand held tight,
Not knowing how else to help her.

In those lonely uncertain spaces,
I learned of love's expression.
Not from sharing comfort's verses,
By simply listening without solution.

And I cried with her
And I hustled with her
And in still moments,

She, in turn, would listen,
Combing her fingers through my hair.
My head lay gently, with affection,
Adrift in love without a care.

Five Hundred Lunches

I knew he was flawed,
Flawed in ways
I never approved.
But I gave and forgave him
His flaws, and
Together we grew, and
Together we worked, and
I learned behavior
I am still learning to unlearn.

And still,
I deeply loved the man, my father.

To my count, we sat
Face-to-face over
Five hundred lunches,
Hundreds of tables,
Thousands of syllables.

Throughout my thirties
Throughout his sixties
My father, he pulled me
Into his world, and
I was happily led.

Our lunches were
Always filling, always
Easy to digest
Until—I couldn't.
Until—they weren't.

And still,
I never lost my appetite.

Now I knuckle in,
Sitting alone,
In a café we've been to
So many times before.

Longing filled with
Gratitude settles my
Middle-aged soul
Under the accumulated
Weight of five hundred lunches.

Season of Fatherhood *(a blessing)*

As dawn filters out the night
revealing color's kaleidoscope,
may the sparkling eyes of our children
awaken in our hearts an abundance of love.

As this time tilts us closest to the sun,
may it also bring us closer to ourselves and
the cosmic providence we feel in the
embrace of our children.

Since before our children were born,
we were connected to fatherhood
through our fathers and theirs
going back through all time.

May we practice grace with ourselves
as we feel the weight of responsibility
to protect and care for the future
fathers and mothers of our shared ancestry.

With the passing of the summer solstice,
we enter a season of fatherhood.
May we awake in the fullness of sunshine, and
cultivate our better selves according to the light.

May we wrap our arms and hearts
around our children. May we laugh and tumble
with them longer than we think we have time for.

May we strive to know our true selves and
share that truth with them, even as our cell phones vibrate.
May we model vulnerability for our children,

sharing the pathway to belonging with others.
May we feel more connected through the light of the sun
shining equally on us all.

May we be grateful for our fathers.

Changing a Man
Prelude to the poem

When I met Remy the wild mustang, he had been gathered from his wild herd in the harsh eastern plains of Oregon only six months prior. I was randomly wandering through a barn on a rainy Puget Sound afternoon, passing time, when I came across Remy in crossties, his deep chestnut coat being clipped by a slight young woman. Her mother sat across the aisle chatting with her, and as I paused to watch, we struck up a conversation. The unbelievable story they shared about Remy caused a new turn of thought to unfold inside my mind. According to the young woman, her hand was the first hand to lay on Remy's shoulder. She'd "gathered" him, claimed him from the herd, and in roughly four months, she was riding him, loading him in and out of a horse trailer, and feeding him handsomely with love and healthy amounts of oats and alfalfa. Remy and his gatherer's story mesmerized me. Remy had no idea that there was any other way to be but with the herd. Left in the wild, Remy, would likely live half as long, and on the edge—one injury, one wildfire, one drought away from death. In his new cultural context, Remy has never been more well-nourished and at peace. That led me to these questions: Is there a better version of the American culture available to me? If so, how do I access or manifest that better cultural paradigm within myself?

Changing a Man

The culture runs the horses wild,
no thought but herd.
A wild rampage no bare soul can bear.
Stampeded into dust until all there is
is soul-barren dust.
Full fear of exposure
until You are forgotten.
The herd has all answers.
The culture runs all horses.

Where is the soul of a man without the spirit?

Feel her hand fall gently on your shoulder,
your awareness expanding to just beyond
the periphery of the herd.
Calling for new truths,
new covenants with creation.
Calling for prayerful grieving.
Keep praying. Keep grieving.
Let go of fear. Let go of shame,
a child is deep within
wanting to be led to love.

Where is the spirit for the soul of a man?

Follow her falling without thinking.
Deep within the darkness
a golden embryo of color
invites you to embrace the question.
When holding only questions,
you can never be wrong.

Our white father ancestors took questions,
raped them, and imposed answers.
Hold only the question,
hold only the question.
Dare to share with her.
Listen quietly, she whispers life.
The spirit is held in the air between.
Inhale.

Within darkness,
the seed of color begins
its slow growth to a new spring.
The indigenous five fingers reaching
through Mother Earth into shared being.
No more answers, only wonder, color, feeling.

The Way is an ancient spirit of fearless generosity.
Inside the spirit, the soul-child of the man resides.

Under Cover

The culture blows the canopy
Of my ego in a desperate display.
Every leaf folding and twisting
I grip firmly for others to see.
Fearful of exposure,
Never questioning letting go.

The wind lashes and whips branches.
In praise of nature, it is time,
Let loose your leaves!
Feel the sinew pull,
The tissue tear—
Release hold.

Each answer falls, a leaf from the canopy.
So many more, so much more,
Until only questions remain as

Darkness descends, and
Color recedes into the cold.
Standing naked and exposed,
This season of earth
Calls me to myself.

The Landing

I felt the sound,
my heart breaking.
A thousand shards skating
across the landing of our home.

It was no accident,
these things never are.
It was an accumulation.
I bent over

to try to gather
and piece it back together.
There were too many
pieces . . . a gathering

of glass rose petals, not a
bouquet, but every memory
a perfect petal,
these things always are.

I feel them like echoes
calling to me
from somewhere unaware to me,
From deep withinside me.

How to comprehend
an echo? A reverberation,
a flicker of the frame.

In time bodies move,
bodies in motion move.
And so, we are moving,
fracturing forward and—

Away.
Now we're intertwining with new
forms and stories with
new bodies, broken,

the color
of pain—
Red petals of glass shards
on the landing.

The blood petals scattered,
we gathered what we could
until there was nothing more
                worth saving.

                        Embedded in the fertile soil of grief
                                fine green shoots

Falling

Falling through
Thin air
Fast

The end
Now Rapidly
Approaching

Back awake
In bed
Grateful

Small stay
From oblivion's
Calling

Falling

Falling

Calling
From oblivion's
Small stay

Grateful
In bed
Back awake

Approaching
Now Rapidly
The end

Fast
Thin Air
Falling through

Falling

Find your way back to yourself

Dark Elements

Prelude to the poem

Friend, our closeness is this:
Anywhere you put your foot, feel me
In the firmness under you.

How is it with this love,
I see your world and not you?

—Rumi

The first time I read this Rumi poem was in college, a ways back. It is a beautiful poem evoking the nature of true friendship. Yet, the paradox at the end of poem has caused me, on many occasions, to reflect with curiosity. How can Rumi love someone so deeply and help carry the weight of their heavy loads, yet still not really see the person? Is he fooling himself? Is that really love? Or is the love Rumi is talking about some form of pseudo-love?

What if Rumi was talking about something else entirely? Who are we so intimately close to, yet still struggle to know and see? Ourselves. Could Rumi be speaking to himself?

Perhaps he recognizes that he is the closest friend he has? Friend, our closeness is this: anywhere you put your foot, feel me in the firmness under you. How amazing!? If he is indeed talking to himself, this is what we all need to feel in terms of self-kindness. To feel ourselves firmly aligned and supportive—and supported. I believe that Rumi was truly practiced in self-compassion; how else could he be!? And he felt his way there! Feel me in the firmness under you. Powerful.

Yet in the second verse, he comes to a sort of confession, asking himself an existential question, how is it with this love, I see your world but not you? In other words, he can see all the manifestations of his body and his world, but he can't clearly see himself. How is this? Rumi is practiced in self-kindness, yet self-knowledge eludes? I believe this to be a truth of the human condition. We may not hate ourselves and can be kind to ourselves from time to time, and yes, we may love ourselves and can therefore love others. However, knowing ourselves—well, that can be a lifelong journey.

The poem that follows is a reflection on Rumi's poem. The mysterious pathway to self-knowledge may be best followed in the same manner as the self-kindness in the first verse of Rumi's poem, through feeling. Perhaps we develop self-knowledge by feeling our way through the darkness of our souls rather than attempting to see?

Dark Elements

Friend, come alive gently in the early darkness.
Walk quietly through the room softly breathing, and
Make your way to the front door.

Don't be afraid.

Grab your bag and place within it
A thermos of warm tea, a sitting pad.
Walk out the front door.

Don't be afraid, you can do it, my friend.

Take a deep breath and enter the forest.
Wander deep into those woods until you hear
Flowing water and sit in darkness.

Do not be afraid, it will be okay.

In time the darkness will fade
Into dim light growing ever green.
Wait for it with eyes closed.

Don't be afraid,

     feel your way,

         you are right
         there.

Running in Silence

I ran on trails
And sat in silence.
The earth shifted.
The ferns trembled.
The sky grew
Dark with clouds.

I kept running on trails,
And sat in silence.
The animals began
Their death throes
Howling overtook
The swirling air.

Running trails
And sitting silently.
Shit stains the carpet.
The dishes pile high.
Dirty laundry spills
Out the door.

Still running still silent still sitting.
But there is
No more running.
No more silence.
No sitting.

Walking beside myself,
I speak to myself:
"Self, same-self, open
Your eyes inward,
See the sirens' song,
Listen to the sun
Rising on the horizon.

You were already on
Your way back to
Yourself without knowing.
Without knowing,
Embrace what you fear to be true–
Hold her earthen head
To your breast.
Move on, keep
Moving on."

Perspective

The mosquito comes to me
for my blood.

The entire life of it!

In the gaps between the
endless cacophony
of the trivial
I can feel the bloodletting.

The prick and pain of it,
the itch.

The itch is an obsession.
Relief comes only
from distraction—

The anesthetic of
attending to the trivial,
gorging on the mass of life
in the pursuit of
immortal pretenses.

Feel the mosquito.

Pandemic Pentameter

Breakfast with a kiss upon your brow,
Served upon the table made with love's
Attention during this uncommon isolation.
We sit together and read in silence.

The daily paper holds the changing rules.
We are told to keep our masks,
To take positions on life and death,
And we fall forward into the unknown.

Pretending not to care too much,
We feel the pressure mount.
Where once we found a common ground,
We now oppose the ones we love.

Joy is in the changing of the season,
In the faith that this too shall pass,
In the closeness of our love,
In the dream this virus will abate,

And in our bliss the parks will fill with
Unmasked inhibition, as we all
Caress each other, and
Learn our names again.

We read the words of rage in fear's debate,
Woven with white anger and protest.
Rebellion breeds in isolation as sides are taken,
And we divide and side with our tribe, online.

Steeped within the daily news,
A numbness seeps within.
While fear, unease, and the trivial,
Barb their thorny lashings to us.

In the quiet morning hour, we sit side by side
And hold with silent knowledge:
No matter our daily pantomime,
This sickness plagues us all.

Husbandry

The time of death became the time.
The husband had been procrastinating.
The march of time, slow as it can be, had left him with the sense
that relationships last forever, that the time may never arrive.
But the time always arrives, and this time he chose the time
to bring death downward.
He chose the hour of separation.

The departed husband, without telling his children,
arranged with the remaining wife to be alone
with death, with the chickens, chickens
that could no longer suffer neglect,
lack of attention, affection, nourishment, love.

The first chicken, the white-lightning-terminator-chicken,
put up a good chase for the husband
until he pinned it against the henhouse:
squawk and squeal, the fluff of feathers flapping,
its wings beat powerfully up against him.

The white bird had escaped the talons of death once before,
when a hawk swooped in and gripped it, and
the husband swung a freighted broom
and the hawk flew away
leaving, fluttering, the chicken's white feathers.

But this time the husband
snapped its neck.
He held the bird firmly under his arm
and leaned against the family fir tree,
the tire-swing he'd hoisted still swaying.
He leaned on that tree and held on through death throes,
breathing compassion over the transition
until the final spasm.

Throwing the white feathered dress to the dirt,
the husband turned inward.
His vile gut churned as his tears made room for
the death of another bird, another bird, another bird—
Death descending with swift surety.
Death at his hands held for all to see.

This Island

On this island
in the middle of a pool
of green grass
between
ripe fruit trees
there is an old picnic table,
wobbly and scarred.
I sit at this table, with
a cup of coffee and my journal

and gaze into a fractal pattern of
black birds twirling
through the air.

I have no control—
I have lost control—
but the table still stands,
the pages of my journal
fill.

Did I have to leave my wife?
Was the death of our relationship required?

Every time I open my
mouth, the sound of
bird song.

When I stand, scarred and wobbly,
from the table,
I am flying high,
spinning
in an avian cyclone—

Descent or ascent,
it makes no matter.
I can only follow the whirl
and trust my emerging wings
as I fly
from this island.

Within Wilderness
for Dan - for Dave - for me

Tiger lily and lupine
Line the trail of our wounded walk.

Footfall after footfall
Forms the cadence of our conversation.

Cool alpine lakes and rivers
Flow into our overheated souls.

Kestrels and Momo Butterflies
Swoop in soothing relief.

Cubs, kids, and their mothers
Mimic our kindred connection.

Heather and Indian paint brush
Color the boundaries of our hearts.

Granite peaks and sprawling meadows
Surround our imaginations.

Trail names and forest magic
Generate the banter between us.

Walking while healing
Within wilderness.

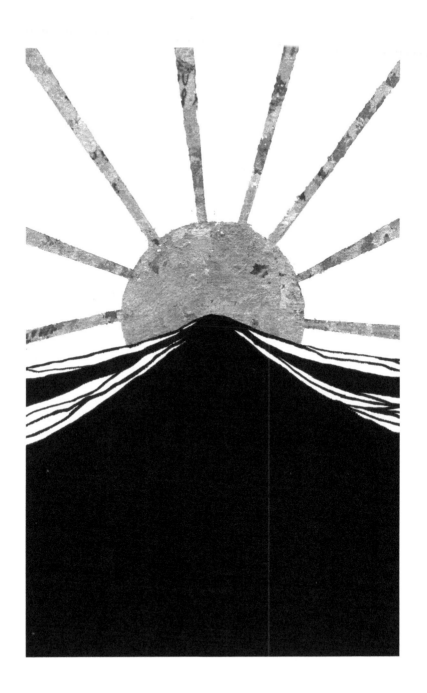

A Solstice Blessing

As the sun appears to stand still
Briefly holding its northernmost turning point,
May you also hold firmly and turn
To peace and the power of renewal,
Allowing the brightest rays of the sun to
Radiate through you.

Under June's Strawberry Moon,
Mother Earth lies
Abundantly fertile,
Absorbing the fullness
Of the sun's healing power.

May you gently, and
With determination,
Leave behind to be burned
What you no longer need.
Feel the fertile healing power
Of the Sun and Earth cultivating
Courage within your soul.

Anything that does not
Bring you alive is to be left behind.

May the Midsummer season
Wax on you with good fortune,
An abundance of growth, and new
Nurturing relationships
Aligned with your emergent future self.

As these new relationships intertwine,
May this season bring them strength and
A deep sense of love and gratitude
Beyond previous seasonal turnings.

And above all, may you find peace in the awareness
That to shine like the sun,
You must first burn like the sun.
To employ the power of the sun to help heal others,
You must first be burned to heal yourself.

Owls of Adventure

I feel you grab and let go
Only after you fly past me.

In your tree, perched above,
You circle me with your roundness.
An invitation in silent motion
To engage in an ancient ballet.

You, with fine ferns for wings,
Circular grain-of-the-wood for eyes,
Nested within the body of old growth.
Me, milky white and tender from
Under shelter and wool cover.

I run uncovered deep
Within your forest.
Do you sense me
Running your way before my
Headlamp emerges, calling
You to flightful banter?
And so the dance begins.

What is this we share
In the twilight forest,
Following your lead, following me?
And I laugh, you are playing with me!
Waltzing me back and forth
Through your wooded ballroom.

Ha Ho!

I am no quarry for your gullet.
I am your playful whimsy.
You move me with your feathery
Forested outstretched wings, and
Watch me run and twirl
Out of my clothes,
Laughing so sanely.

Bears of Adventure
Prelude to the poem

I have done a fair bit of trail running in the hills around my home. The wilderness forest of the Central Cascades fingers into the edge developments where I live. As a result, I have on many exciting occasions run into bears on the trail. And not just bears! Coyote, owl, bobcat, deer, raccoon, and more have crossed my path at some point during my time on trails. When writing this poem, I spent a bit of extra time considering bears. They are often viewed as the mystical mega-fauna of this region. Most bear species—but not all—hibernate. Upon further investigation I learned that the black bear can hibernate up to seven and a half months of the year. Think about that! Black bears are dreaming in hibernation for more than half of their lives. When they are not hibernating, they still sleep and dream at night. Black bears live the majority of their lives in the land of their dreams! Perhaps our understanding of their mystic quality resides within this question: How does a bear know when it's not dreaming?

Bears of Adventure

I hear the forest break as you pass through, before
You amble-cross my path, and I see you.

You are unaware and dream-walking,
All nose with dim eyes and ears up, listening.

Bristle-black pine needles for hair,
You are unique and every bear.

From one to another, a mystic relation,
Born thru half a life dreaming in hibernation.

You come to a standstill, your nose in the air,
Attempting to confirm I'm actually there, and

Halfway between your dream and the air,
Between your nose and me, a whiff of reality.

You are simply following smell!
I am resisting the urge to yell,

"Hey bear!"

Am I in a dream you are walking through?
Now you stare at me, "Is it true?"

Yes, a human, a scent of what's known . . .
I grasp for my camera phone.

Are we dreaming together?!

When floating through a bear-dream,
Daytime is often not what is seen.

If we are dreaming, or if this is real,
A photograph will clearly reveal, but

In disbelief you shake your bristlecone,
Yawn your blades, taste tongue to nose, and

Wander forward in lucid dreamtime,
Before I can focus, to leave me in mine.

Sandpiper

Sandpiper, sandpiper

Fine and refined.

You flick and twitch.
Peck and stitch.

Scurry-hurry
In a flurry
To the murky tideline.

Back again, back again.

Find your friend, find your friend.
Down on the shoreline
And up again, up again.

On dry sand

You twirl around, whirl around.
Spin around, and fly—

To another patch

You poke and scratch

For your morning...

Splash! a wave!

Pelican,
the Other Worlds

Gliding seamless just above
A deep and unknown fathom,
Whose timeless mystery's trove
Contain a universal quantum.

Your wingtip, without knowing,
Cuts through the surface below
Revealing a hidden opening
Into an infinite tomorrow.

The ancient ocean spans before you,
Providing all you need.
Secrets held within the deep blue
Make an endless well within to feed.

Unaware of this connection, you glide
With the wind, up and over the endless tide.

Post-script to the poem
The question underlying this poem is: If it is
true that a pelican holds a working under-
standing of the surface layer of the ocean,
but knows or understands nothing of the
profound and expansive world of water and
creatures in the depths beneath its wingtips,
can I be so sure there are no worlds of the
unknown around me?

Doe Eyes

She stares
Into my glowing headlamp, transfixed.

Such beauty in her silky elegance,
Immovable in her silver refinement, she is
Poised in herself
Within the elements we share.

I stare
Into her glowing eyes, transfixed.

That beauty we share.
Unmoving on the edge of time,
Poised in falling water, we are
Embodied together within the elements, one

Beating and breathing animal, in still motion.

Wild Blueberries

While wandering wilderness waterways,
Looking for holes harboring trout,
I find bushes of puffy
Deep purple blueberries

Filling the wooded
Sun-dappled hillside
Along the river's edge.

So, I sit and pick plump wild berries.
My hand makes a cup, and
All-in-one

Into my grinning mouth!

Juices squish and press and squeeze:
Sweetness and seeds throughout my mouth.
I pick another cup, another cup
Another cup.

Octaves of rushing water
Surround and drown my thoughts
Into purple picking fingers, and
Not much else

But: fish are only caught
with a line in the water!

But: the blueberry juices are
... squishing ... me

Hand as cup,
as cup
as cup
cup

I am resigned
To wandering, and
To nothing, save
Blueberries.

Illusions of Mind

I tell myself to throw aside the well-made plan and suffer
the inconvenience of not receiving what I think I want.
Will what I want in this moment make me happy in the next?

The trickling brook of thought flows through
one off-shoot and into whirling eddies:
Why one way and not the other?

Who am I to believe I know
what will come next to mind, or
if my flowing thoughts lead true?

If you jump in my river of thought
will it flow true
for you too?

Blue Heron

Poised in your elegance
With feathery jewels draping
The slender sculpture of your curving neck.

Your stillness invites
All of time to pour into the
Moment your position commands.

Held high
Above the gentle surf
On thin and stately legs,
Your royal prowess
Captures my imagination.

Then the slow but sure
Motion of your craning attention
Releases time's hold with a flash and precision—

A fish found suddenly wiggling in your bill!

Urgency
–After Sengcan

The Way is smooth flowing water.
It enables through
Easy and difficult times,
Always the same.
But all minds become distracted.
And many, lost.
Rushing to get ahead,
They fall behind and have
Already begun to wither.

Holding It All

As the sun rises on the
Landscape of tomorrow,
It sets on the
Horizon of yesterday,
Forever closing
Into an eternal opening—

There is no space
To fall between.

Yet stillness beckons,
And awareness blows into
The warm air of thought,
Rising above the turning times,
And in the thin air of altitude
I feel the vast mystery, the
Beauty and terror of it all,

And smile.

To Bear

Standing tall,
taller still,
with stiff black hair
standing high—

At the highest point
of the highest place
on the bridge
I can't stop
running to cross—

The black bear
of my shrouded fear
stands there.

Should I be afraid?
That is the question
with bears.

The Cabin on Gold Creek

Darkness, and an unforgiving freeze
presses against the cabin's walls.

Inside, the living is warm, a stew
simmers on the woodstove,
goodness itself wafting on waves of
warmth from the fire.
                    Outside,
hostile extremes seem to swirl
from distant and unseen forces

while inside, the animals lounge
around the hearth, and guitars
deliver the evening news.

Pandemic, death panels, protests, and war—
they drift in on drafts through cracks between the logs
and swirl into the ephemeral—

We fill our cups again, music, hot stew,
our company become the
nonsense news within.

Open Road

I grip the wheel and go
with the traffic on
the crowded highway,
eastbound into the sun.

Hemmed in by
brush-by drivers,
their beady eyes
flash side to side.

The mountains stand still
in silent witness
above the polluted
river of madness.

Nothing grips but
fear and rage.
The hovering clouds
distract from a deep blue sky.

Open road,
Open road, goddamnit!
Open road—

What I need.

Behold

And I, in the desire of men,
Cast my eye upon her.

Behold: love longing
To be light and playful.
She is wrapped within her children,
Holding them tight to the
Breast of love.

She is breathing deeply,
Balanced to pose.
Her eyes piercing uncertainty.
Daring her dreams
To not come true.

She is agile, eros in motion.
Water in sunshine, moon in fire.
Navigating barefoot
Through never-ending
Forests the future forward.

And I, with the desire of men,
Place my hand on the
Back of her head,
Gently tilting the world
With a kiss upon her neck.

When Waiting

What is it with waiting?
Waiting in the lobby to be seen,
Waiting in the line of
Everything, of life,
That causes the squirm of
Anxiety to wiggle within us?

Put the phone down from
Distracting yourself from
Yourself.

Now, hold the space
and hum a tune,
Watch your wandering mind.
Feel the tune, its vibration,
and focus on that feeling.

Relax the wiggle away.

Forever Man

When the Woman arrives,
All of thought and feeling floods.

From where, to what, why?

Follow the thought
Back in time, and
You will find
Your ancestors
Reflecting in the pool
Back at you.

Undercurrents

Balancing, but not balanced.
Feeling, but not felt.
Looking, but not seeing.
Sensed, but not understood.

So often, without knowing,
From dark depths rising,
Messages arrive without words.
Ciphers of the heart.

A Together Solitude

And here we are, each
within ourselves.

You, all alone
within yourself
        next to me
all alone within mine.

You are now

sharing your all-alone-self
        next to mine,
for us to see and be
one within another

together

within this music, and the
forever-raging storm that
pulls the flames from the oven
up the stovepipe with the

incense of this love
swirling into the cyclone.
Two hearts merging
for a time into one.

Of Running Desire

A high-gear coyote
bursts onto the trail
racing right in front of me—

trees heavy from
an evening of warm rain
lie limp across the path.

Bare-chested and running,
wet limbs and leaves
lick and kiss my torso.

Red breasted robins
In lust chirping tones
flutter along the trail.

The idea of feathers
swells my wet skin.
Desire for her everywhere . . .

Black Light
Prelude to the poem

My journey of white self-discovery, wrapped as it is within the American cultural context, has been difficult and enlightening. The most remarkable aspect of the journey has been the enlightenment I have received from my African American brothers and sisters who have shined their light on me, our shared past, and on the vision of a beloved community. I call their light the Black Light. It's the ultraviolet light that helps me see the truth of our past, our present, and the possibility of a future free of racism and white supremacy.

When the Black Light, the ultraviolet light, shines on our interwoven ancestry, it reveals the stain of racism still woven within the structures of society today. When my fragility can take the heightened vision no longer, I close my eyes off to the Black Light and recede back into the monochromatic white-supremacist, status-quo-culture, the paradigm, and I return to living my unaware life as a privileged white man in America.

Yet, when I am open, and the Black Light strobes on my eyes and heart again, I see still more racism in painful hidden messages woven into mainstream American culture—woven into me. Over time I have learned to adjust my sight, and more often I'm able to see the racism in the American culture—and in me—more clearly.

I also see possibility. When the Black Light shines on the journey forward, it reveals the beautiful potential that is available to all of us: a beloved kaleidoscopic community of people aware of
their interconnectedness and the central ingredient of love.

America's culture was founded on the belief of white supremacy. In so doing the culture wrongly marginalized everyone else and created the concept of — "the marginalized." African American brothers and sisters, our family of the First Nations in the Americas, and all those who have been defined as "marginalized" because they are not white—seem to me to be able to see the full spectrum of colors on our cultural canvas most clearly. The ability to transform the culture is accessible only to those who can clearly see the racist stains in our shared ancestry—and the highest potential in our shared future.

I acknowledge the enslavement, genocide, oppression, and the role my ancestors and I have played in creating a white supremist culture. I am regretful and I am grateful—grateful for all the people, past and present, that have had the courage, endurance, willingness, and patience, to help me improve my own vision, internally and externally, past and future.

Black Light

Black Light

There is a stain I can't see,
Not even within me.
As a young man
Not yet knowing
The true fabric of life.
White, yet not yet white.
Unfolding into whiteness
Without awareness.
It all made sense,
Yet, it does not yet
Make sense.
Not knowing
What not holding
Power is
When holding
Power, yet
Not wanting
Power over.

Black-Light

There is a stain I can't see
Walking in a world
With perfect clarity.
Born free into
A white male body.
Born in America
As a priority.
Walking through
A sea of opportunity
Designed for me.
It all makes sense
In the land of the free
Designed for me.

Black-Light

There is a stain I can't see
Yet, how to make sense of
Senseless uplifting struc-
tures
I hold
That others do not
          "Naturally"
                    Hold?

Black-Light

There is a stain I *won't* see
Being revealed to me. But,
My work is a priority, and
My family validates me.
What does this stain
Mean to me?
How can there be
When I *earned*
my opportunity?
Maybe others aren't
as smart as me, or
Work as hard as me?
What does this stain
really mean to *me?*

Black-Light

There is a stain I think I see
Even withinside of me.
I've learned it is a stain of
ultra-violent hierarchy,
That has brought
Opportunity to me,
That others
        "Naturally"
                    see.
What does this stain

Mean for me?

Black-Light

There is a stain I see
Withinside of me.
A middle-aged man
Learning the true
Fabric of life.
White, yet not wanting
white,
Yet, not knowing how.
With awareness,
It all makes sense.
Yet, it does not yet
Make sense.
Now knowing
What holding
Power is
When holding
Power, yet
Not wanting

Power
Over.

Black Light

There is a beauty
I now see.
A new future
Being revealed to me.
A vision of
Beloved Community.
Together we weave
At the loom
Our future history.
A color-filled tapestry
Telling a story of
Shared ancestry.
I can now see,
Weaving within me
Shared threads
Weaving together
To shine... shiney... shine—
With the beauty of the
Black light shining on
And never shining off
                again.

Black Light
Black Light
Black Light
Black Light
Black Light
Black Light
Black Light...

Owning It

If they take aim in my town,
    Defending their way of life,
        Confederated throughout,

They will look for the other, and me too
    If they knew I was other, but
        I can get by in my privilege.

Which is
    To say
        My skin.

Which is
    To ask
        Will I walk between them?

        The duty of my privilege demands that I do.

But
    Will
        I?

Flowing Together

Wandering together with minds wide and open hearts,
our ideas interplay, unfolding in thin air,
ephemeral flutterings of figuring.

One wonders, and then another,
one leads, and then another
one questions, and then
a bloom of thought forms

a feeling. Called to life, the
felt form takes shape,
a ghostly image for the eyes
of more than one mind to see.

An improvisation from nothing
into a mental silhouette that flows from feeling
to seeing, to silky allure, and back again while
wandering together with minds wide and open hearts.

Within a River Bend

Sitting outside in a stone pew sanctuary,
All the eyes of the gathering are
Oriented toward me, and
A silence takes hold inside.

I am mindful,
  A soft breeze tickles my skin . . .
    We

      swam gently, flowing
        water soothed our skin
      caught disks of laughter
        in the sunshine
      explored questions along pathways
        lined with hearts of gold
      dreamt around glowing embers
        in the darkness
      tasted the rich
        marrow of connection.

And suddenly, here we are,
Sitting silently together
Looking into each other,

Exposing our fear of being seen.

  We are only human beings.
    Gratefully . . .

The Weight of Love
Prelude to the poem

To live and love authentically is to experience heartbreak. Heartbreak is simply part of the deal with love; with love comes the rip and tear of heartbreak. Unfortunately, it is within that very rip and tear where new growth wants to emerge. And this is so painful. And this simply is.

The Weight of Love
For Billy and Corrina

When I enter
the forest interior
after the snow recedes,
the sword ferns are flattened
and leveled from the white
weight melted away the week before.

No fern was spared the immensity.
Stalks smashed and leaves bent upside down,
their light green underbellies signaling submission.

Is it the way of love's quiet
and accumulating density
—surprising us with such creeping intensity—

that causes our own interior forests
to become
compressed and torn?

Is it so space can be made within
the tear of blade and sinew
for new life to swell in the body
of the world again?

From the Beyond,
...Walt Mink

A settling will eventually arrive.

My death, your friend.

A mystery I cannot resolve for you.

But know that after celebration,
A good mourning will
Soak into your soul.

And with sufficient saturation, you will feel
A free
      fall
      forward.
Solace will seep into your heart and
My mortality will be confirmed.

Warped within a restless wake,
A musical reverb.
Your fingers will burn to bleeding.
You will pour beer onto the earth.
Your howling will bridge
To a universe in silence.

Alone, lying on top of that ridge
You still feel my wake.
The infinite expanding space
Viewed in rare depth.
My gift to you from the beyond.

Friend, the shimmering cosmos
Calls to us all . . . . .

Settle into hopelessness,
Free from mortality.

Mink's Haiku

Divorced and alone
He walked to a silent field
Planting figurines

Forever Forested
–for Dan for Chuck for Calvin

Did the rainforest hear it coming?
Did the elder trees brace for impact?
Did the cold river bend in anticipation?
Did the night owls hoot warnings?
Did the draping moist moss part ways?

When the car finally broke through,
Violently falling, hissing and
Steaming, into the night waters,
Did the forest inhale the son's pain, and
Exhale life into the surrounding silence?

Did the trees maintain their compassionate hold?
Did the river warmly work its way heart-ward?
Did the night owls coo a soothing sound?
Did the cool moss drape across his forehead?
Did the rainforest feel the pain and the release?
Did it welcome the boy lovingly to the other shore?

The flowers floating downstream said it was so.

Mas
–for Alan

We settled around and placed our hands on the hound.
Three men patting through thick red fur.
He lived, sleeping mostly, in the middle of the room
      for several days,
His pack of dogs and men moving about him.

Loretta the puppy, just a couple months old,
Alternated between snuggling in
And chewing on his back leg––
      she sensed he was deathward.

Labored breathing, an occasional wheeze,
Just the day before we were able to steady him outside.
He lifted his leg without lifting,
      and then
On his pillow again in the house of his final resting.

His day came the day following.
Gaunt, his labored breathing
      held a rapid heart,
His eyes remained alive to the room and us in it—
Three men patting and rubbing his thick red fur.

The weight of him in his pillow was easy.
We carried him up to the grave we'd dug
      earlier in the day,
A bottle of whiskey on the ground,
A rifle propped on the dirt mound,
We held back while Alan gently
      rested the rifle barrel behind his ear.

When the gun fired, I broke and placed my hand on his seizing body.
"Good boy, Mas. I feel you going now. Good boy."
We all rubbed his fur, passed the bottle, told stories,
cried and laughed, and then
We lowered the red furry body of the hound into the ground.

                No Mas . . .

Departure

One final visit to a dawn-drenched shore.
One last longing look.
One last listen.
One last surge.

The constant tide drums a cosmic rhythm.
My ears.
My chest.
My being.

Between me and the thin line of horizon,
an azure underworld of mystery.
My eyes.
My mind.
My soul.

One final morning to soak it all in.
To carry it with my fragility.
To carry it out from within.
To carry, to carry it.

The Warm Roof-Deck

The wind carries the
Essence of ocean as
My imagination rides the
Current out to the horizon.

With every lip and curl
Of the swell,
I inhale and exhale the
Sound of tide.

As I climb the staircase to
A warm roof deck,
The outlook expands
Into a forever navy blue.

Clouds light the edge
of space.

They offer me a question.

Can I answer it?

Can I be more grateful to have lived
Than resentful of the day when I lose it all?

The Source

My father died this day one year ago.
Now that he is ended
I consider,
Where did he begin?
I go in search of the source.

Running in the rain
Along turquoise whitewashed rivers,
Through ancient groves, elders, generations,
I go in search of the source.

Along a trail carved with history
To hot springs of hope—
Water, pure, flowing
From within the earth.
Fragrance of earth's interior.
Of sulfur's burning.
I go in search of the source.

Naked into the water I go—
A cave opens within the darkness,
Chest-deep—my skin
Becomes electric within.
At the far end of the cave,
A shadow emerges as if
Hovering along the dark water's edge.
It descends
Into
The hot water,
Merging with me, with the water.
The source?

Gliding through the rippling waters
Deeper into the darkness.
Feeling for the ledge at the far end,
I climb out, lie down, and
Look out through the entrance
Opening into the world.

Am I the source?

Questions multiplied on the journey:
Sounds of flowing water, echoing voices.
Into the earth I descended
And I waded out in wonder,
This dark source

I am.

Acknowledgements

First, I would like to thank my community of friends, my chosen family, my family, my work/ playmates, mentors and guides and coaches, pastors, and gurus, alive and dead, who have influenced me and allowed me to be here. I am deeply grateful for your contribution to my being. What a privilege to have learned from all of you!

Thank you, Susan, for all the years, for the love, and for generously giving me the space to embark on this journey. Thanks to my children, Mia and Bodhyn, for so much inspiration and your never-ending curiosity. You have helped me maintain the clarity of childhood sight and insight. And Mom, your support and never-ending love and kindness will always be felt and remembered.

Thank you, Dan. Your writing has always pushed me to be a better writer. The strength of our friendship, like granite. More mountains! Speaking mountains, Alan and Chris—fellas, thank you for always inspiring mountains within me. You guys taught me how to climb, ski, adventure outdoors and to become a man better off with a guitar in hand before any of us knew these things. Willis, thank you for being a loyal friend, a mountain adventurer, a thought wrestler and full of laughter. Remember when we were in Africa!? Nicko—thank you for always jesting and checking in; your punches of levity often smack me off guard and out of the oh-so-seriousness of it all. Samuel L, it is hard to imagine the other life I would be living without you as my brother. Thank you for your never-ending kindness and compassion. Our relationship has spanned seasons of our lives, and we have grown in so many parallel ways—how is it you seem to grow younger and wiser at the same time!?—Thank you for always being there. When you didn't have the time or space to share with me, you always seemed to find some of both tucked away just for me.

Karen, thank you for listening and sharing, and for your editorial review. Our many walks, wandering neighborhoods with joints in hand, rooted so much inspiration within these pages. Kyle, we have traveled together through thick and thin pathways. At times I am behind, and you have always been there, often waiting patiently for me to arrive. Thank you for your friendship and kindness. Caleb, you are absolutely the best listener and supporter of my poetry—I am so grateful for all our conversations on work, life, and of course the many poems found in this book. Bishop, you are the man: my brother from another mother; you wouldn't know it, but the pages of this book would be far fewer without our friendship. Thank you for your encouragement and for your trust in me, for seeing into my heart.

Jen, my sister! You have inspired so much goodness in me and the world. Thank you for sharing your surrender experience with mine and for all the banter and the love. Yo! To all the men of WMRJ—thank you for our brotherhood of belonging and our shared passage to the other shore that we will explore throughout the rest of our lives. Thus far the journey has been empowering and transformative. Many of the lines in this book would simply not exist without the experience of our shared journey. Thank you for your kindness and care! Johnny D, thank you for your assistance, support, and care—this book may never have made it to existence without your help. DC, you tap a deep current. Thank you for all the banter and fun forward.

Kary Wayson, you are an inspirational poet of poets. Everyone should read your poetry! You offered me courage and belief in my writing ability when I was listing on my side. Thank you for holding that space. Your brilliance at uncovering the essence—in your own poetry and in mine— has helped me more deeply understand what is possible with words.

Lexy, I am grateful for our work together over the years. I was so stoked to share with you the moment of finding the title of this book! Your simplicity is beauty.

Krystal, you were my first office poetry buddy. Thank you for sharing in the fun. The Secret Trail Poetry Society! Thank you for being my thought partner and forever friend.

Yağmur Kuzay, I want everyone to buy your artwork! Your work connects me to the infinite universe internally and externally. It represents the transformation of being we all experience and has influenced my thinking as I put this book together. Thank you for sharing your artistic insights with me, this book, and the world.

Lastly, I would like to acknowledge that all these poems were conceived directly or indirectly on and through the occupied ancestral homelands of the Coast Salish Peoples, and specifically the Duwamish Tribe. The Duwamish ceded 54,000 acres to the US Government and still have not received reservation land or federal recognition. For tens of thousands of years prior to recorded history they sustained upon the land through their cultural wisdom, perseverance, and innovation. A percentage of the proceeds from the sale of this book will be contributed here: https://www.realrentduwamish.org, in the form of a land tax. Please feel free to consider the ancestral legacies of the lands you occupy. To learn more about voluntary land taxes to the First Peoples please visit this site: https://nativegov.org/news/voluntary-land-taxes/.

About the Author

Poetry entered my journey through the energetic and engaging efforts of my high school English teacher, Gary Plano. Beginning with Coleridge's "Kubla Khan," I have traveled a range of poetry and poets, and I'm grateful there is still so much more to read and learn! Along the journey I've sought to align my life, experiences, and unique skill sets (writing, banking, construction, etc.) with my passion to create a positive environmental and social impact during my short life. In the pursuit of positive impact, I have sought to better understand how to navigate change and transformation. Exploring, writing, and creating frameworks to help people and organizations positively manage change and transformation has been a rewarding pursuit in my life and work at Green Canopy NODE, a company I first conceived in 2008 and help run today. With the aid of many like-minded people, I passionately pursue Green Canopy NODE's mission to build homes, relationships, and businesses to help regenerate communities and environment.

Learn more and connect with Aaron at:
aaronfairchild.com

About the Artist

Yağmur Kuzay is an artist, illustrator, and fashion designer based in Seattle, Washington. Whether it's rock climbing or mountaineering, Yağmur draws her inspiration from her adventures in the great outdoors. Her designs are embodiments of the courage and determination she attempts to bring to every adventure.

Designed by nomadic Creative Director Alexa Ashley
Edited by award-winning, Seattle-based poet, Kary Wayson
Watercolor artwork by Pacific Northwest artist, Yağmur Kuzay
Typeset in Garamond Premier Pro in 9.5, 11 & 13.1pts
J. Ryder Press © 2023 All Rights Reserved
Printed by IngramSpark